ENGLISH

By **Gillian Howell**

RISING STARS

Rising Stars UK Ltd, 22 Grafton Street, London W1S 4EX

www.risingstars-uk.com

This edition 2007

Cover design: Burville-Riley Design
Design: David Blundell, Branford Graphics
Editorial: Deborah Kespert
Illustrations: Phill Burrows

British Library Cataloguing in Publication Data
A CIP record for this book is available from the British Library.

ISBN: 978-1-84680-116-7

Printed by Craft Print International Ltd, Singapore

Acknowledgements
p50 Extract from *The Wind Singer* by William Nicholson.
Text copyright © 2000 William Nicholson. Published by Egmont UK Ltd and used with permission.

p 48 Extract from Key Stage 2 English tests, Reading Test, May 2007.
Reprinted courtesy of the Qualifications and Curriculum Authority.
© Qualifications and Curriculum Authority 2007.

p52 Extract from *Great Expectations* by Charles Dickens. Reproduced courtesy of Marshall Cavendish Ltd.

Contents

How to use this book

Writing fiction and non-fiction

1. **Definition** – This section explains the genre and provides examples of the text type.
2. **Text plan** – Each type of writing is explained step by step to help you plan. Planning is very important when writing fiction and non-fiction, and these charts will help you to plan properly. You are given planning time in the tests, so make sure you use it.

   This icon indicates this is a teaching section.
3. **Language features** – This section explains the typical language used for this type of text, and gives examples.
4. **Explore!** – This section challenges you to find features contained in the text example.
5. **Survival tip** – Key hints and tips to help you achieve a Level 3.
6. **Text example** – This gives you an example of a well-written piece of text that follows the text plan and contains the key language features.
7. **Practice questions** – This is where you do the work. Try answering the questions by using the text plan and by referring to the key language features. Compare it against the written example. Is your answer good enough for a Level 3?
8. **How did you do?** – Read the questions. Can you answer 'yes' to each one?

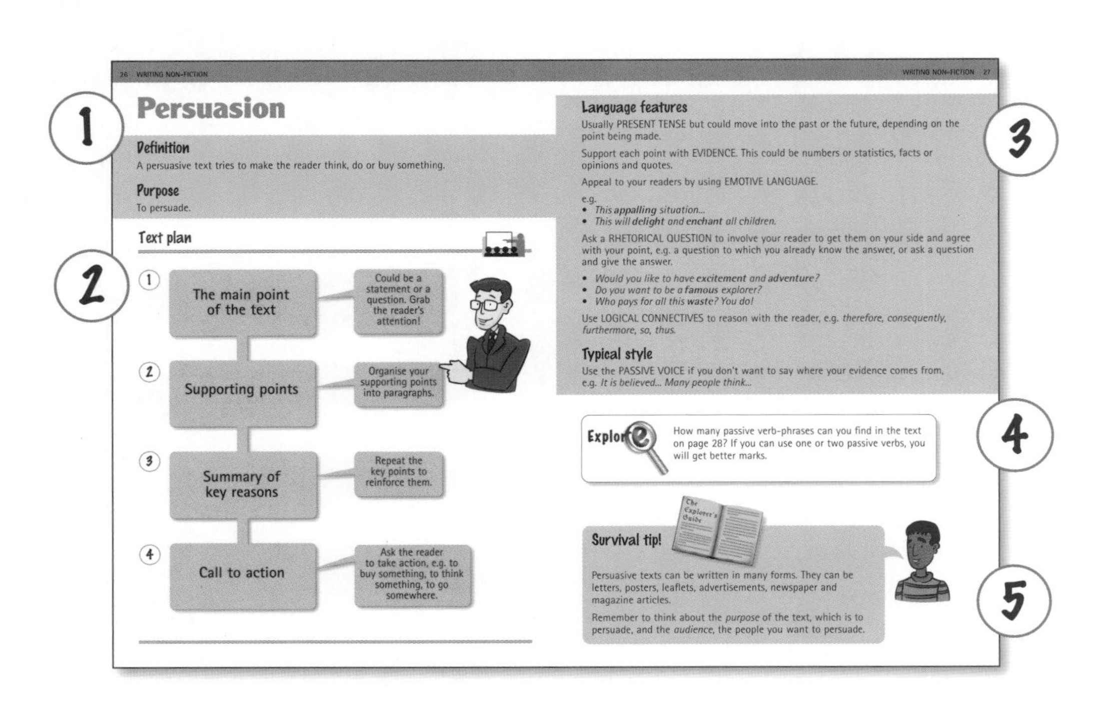

26 WRITING NON-FICTION

Persuasion

Definition
A persuasive text tries to make the reader think, do or buy something.

Purpose
To persuade.

Text plan

1. The main point of the text – Could be a statement or a question. Grab the reader's attention!
2. Supporting points – Organise your supporting points into paragraphs.
3. Summary of key reasons – Repeat the key points to reinforce them.
4. Call to action – Ask the reader to take action, e.g. to buy something, to think something, to go somewhere.

WRITING NON-FICTION 27

Language features
Usually PRESENT TENSE but could move into the past or the future, depending on the point being made.

Support each point with EVIDENCE. This could be numbers or statistics, facts or opinions and quotes.

Appeal to your readers by using EMOTIVE LANGUAGE.

e.g.
- *This **appalling** situation...*
- *This will **delight** and **enchant** all children.*

Ask a RHETORICAL QUESTION to involve your reader to get them on your side and agree with your point, e.g. a question to which you already know the answer, or ask a question and give the answer.

- *Would you like to have **excitement** and **adventure**?*
- *Do you want to be a **famous** explorer?*
- *Who pays for all this **waste**? You do!*

Use LOGICAL CONNECTIVES to reason with the reader, e.g. *therefore, consequently, furthermore, so, thus.*

Typical style
Use the PASSIVE VOICE if you don't want to say where your evidence comes from, e.g. *It is believed... Many people think...*

Explore
How many passive verb-phrases can you find in the text on page 28? If you can use one or two passive verbs, you will get better marks.

Survival tip!
Persuasive texts can be written in many forms. They can be letters, posters, leaflets, advertisements, newspaper and magazine articles.

Remember to think about the *purpose* of the text, which is to persuade, and the *audience*, the people you want to persuade.

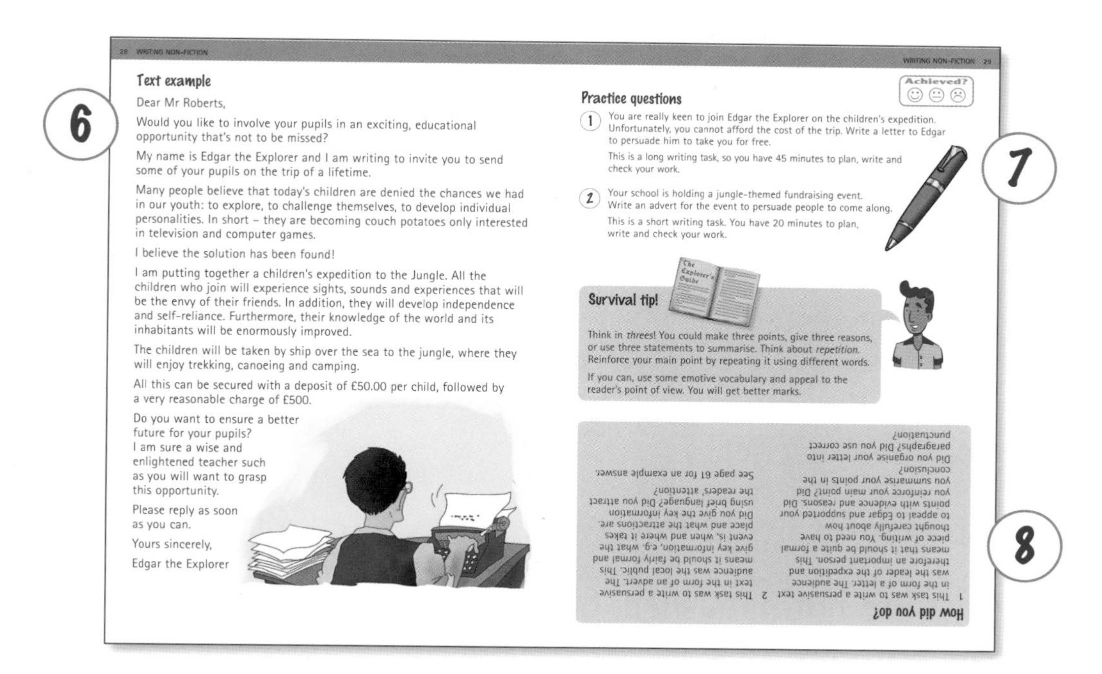

28 WRITING NON-FICTION

Text example

Dear Mr Roberts,

Would you like to involve your pupils in an exciting, educational opportunity that's not to be missed?

My name is Edgar the Explorer and I am writing to invite you to send some of your pupils on the trip of a lifetime.

Many people believe that today's children are denied the chances we had in our youth: to explore, to challenge themselves, to develop individual personalities. In short – they are becoming couch potatoes only interested in television and computer games.

I believe the solution has been found!

I am putting together a children's expedition to the Jungle. All the children who join will experience sights, sounds and experiences that will be the envy of their friends. In addition, they will develop independence and self-reliance. Furthermore, their knowledge of the world and its inhabitants will be enormously improved.

The children will be taken by ship over the sea to the jungle, where they will enjoy trekking, canoeing and camping.

All this can be secured with a deposit of £50.00 per child, followed by a very reasonable charge of £500.

Do you want to ensure a better future for your pupils? I am sure a wise and enlightened teacher such as you will want to grasp this opportunity.

Please reply as soon as you can.

Yours sincerely,

Edgar the Explorer

WRITING NON-FICTION 29

Practice questions

Achieved?

1. You are really keen to join Edgar the Explorer on the children's expedition. Unfortunately, you cannot afford the cost of the trip. Write a letter to Edgar to persuade him to take you for free.

   This is a long writing task, so you have 45 minutes to plan, write and check your work.

2. Your school is holding a jungle-themed fundraising event. Write an advert for the event to persuade people to come along.

   This is a short writing task. You have 20 minutes to plan, write and check your work.

Survival tip!

Think in *threes*! You could make three points, give three reasons, or use three statements to summarise. Think about *repetition*. Reinforce your main point by repeating it using different words.

If you can, use some emotive vocabulary and appeal to the reader's point of view. You will get better marks.

How did you do?

1. This task was to write a persuasive text in the form of a letter. The audience was the leader of the expedition and therefore an important person. This means that it should be quite a formal piece of writing. You need to have thought carefully about how to appeal to Edgar and supported your points with evidence and reasons. Did you reinforce your main point? Did you summarise your points in the conclusion? Did you organise your letter into paragraphs? Did you use correct punctuation?
2. This task was to write a persuasive text in the form of an advert. The audience was the local public. This means it should be fairly formal and give key information, e.g. what the event is, when and where it takes place and what the attractions are. Did you give the key information using brief language? Did you attract the readers' attention?

See page 61 for an example answer.

Reading comprehension

1 Text example – This gives you an example of a text that you might find in your SATs.

2 Questions – There are 1-, 2- and 3-mark questions, so remember for more marks you need to include more in your answer.

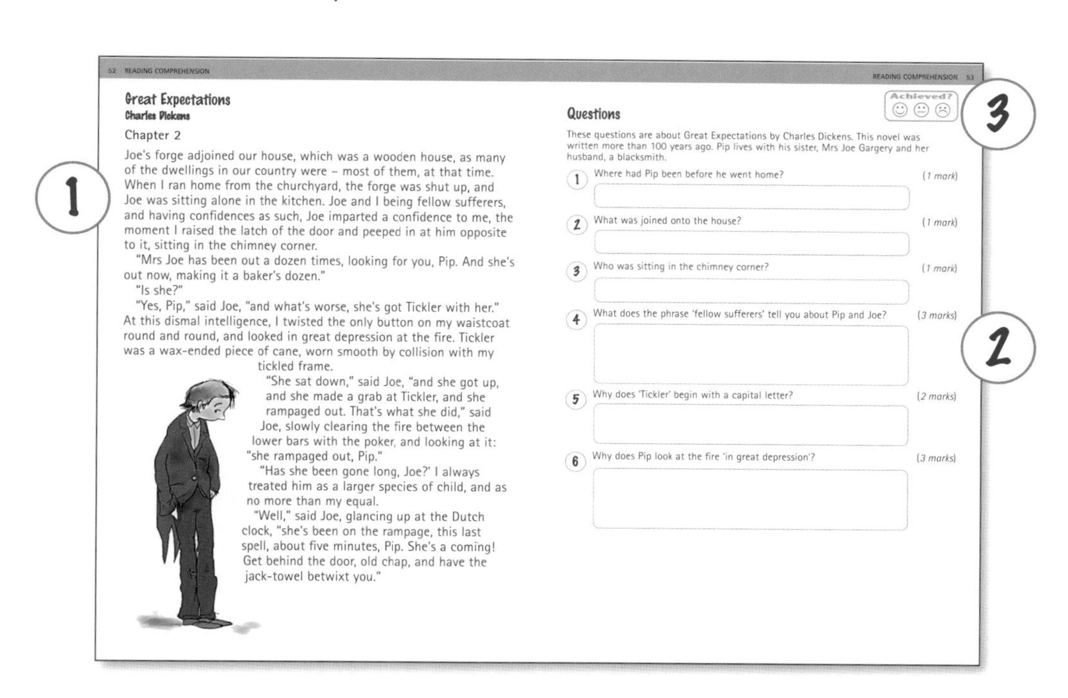

52 READING COMPREHENSION

Great Expectations
Charles Dickens

Chapter 2

Joe's forge adjoined our house, which was a wooden house, as many of the dwellings in our country were – most of them, at that time. When I ran home from the churchyard, the forge was shut up, and Joe was sitting alone in the kitchen. Joe and I being fellow sufferers, and having confidences as such, Joe imparted a confidence to me, the moment I raised the latch of the door and peeped in at him opposite to it, sitting in the chimney corner.

"Mrs Joe has been out a dozen times, looking for you, Pip. And she's out now, making it a baker's dozen."

"Is she?"

"Yes, Pip," said Joe, "and what's worse, she's got Tickler with her." At this dismal intelligence, I twisted the only button on my waistcoat round and round, and looked in great depression at the fire. Tickler was a wax-ended piece of cane, worn smooth by collision with my tickled frame.

"She sat down," said Joe, "and she got up, and she made a grab at Tickler, and she rampaged out. That's what she did," said Joe, slowly clearing the fire between the lower bars with the poker, and looking at it: "she rampaged out, Pip."

"Has she been gone long, Joe?' I always treated him as a larger species of child, and as no more than my equal.

"Well," said Joe, glancing up at the Dutch clock, "she's been on the rampage, this last spell, about five minutes, Pip. She's a coming! Get behind the door, old chap, and have the jack-towel betwixt you."

READING COMPREHENSION 53

Questions

Achieved?

These questions are about Great Expectations by Charles Dickens. This novel was written more than 100 years ago. Pip lives with his sister, Mrs Joe Gargery and her husband, a blacksmith.

1. Where had Pip been before he went home? *(1 mark)*
2. What was joined onto the house? *(1 mark)*
3. Who was sitting in the chimney corner? *(1 mark)*
4. What does the phrase 'fellow sufferers' tell you about Pip and Joe? *(3 marks)*
5. Why does 'Tickler' begin with a capital letter? *(2 marks)*
6. Why does Pip look at the fire 'in great depression'? *(3 marks)*

3 Self-assessment

At the end of each topic, you will see this assessment panel. Colour in the face that best describes your overall understanding of the topic and how you did in your practice.

The National Tests

Key facts

★ The Key Stage 2 National Tests (or SATs) take place in the middle of May in Year 6. You will be tested on Maths, English and Science.

★ The tests take place in your school but are then sent away to be marked by examiners – not your teacher!

★ You usually get your results in July, two months after you take the tests.

★ Individual results are not published, but your school's total results are published in the autumn.

The English National Tests

You will take three tests in English – the Reading Test, the Writing Test and the Spelling Test. Your handwriting is assessed through the Writing Test.

The Writing Test

The Writing Test is made up of two tasks – one shorter task (about 20 minutes) and one longer task (about 45 minutes). Remember to keep your handwriting neat.

The Short Writing Task is 20 minutes long. You should plan briefly, for no longer than two to three minutes, using the prompts. Remember, you have only 20 minutes in total, but you still need to include a one-minute check at the end.

The Long Writing Task is 45 minutes long. You should plan for ten minutes at the most. You must use the plan you are given. However, your planning sheet will not be marked, so you do not need to be neat. Remember, ALWAYS spend three to five minutes at the end for rereading and checking.

The Reading Test

This is one single task to assess your reading comprehension. It lasts about one hour. In this task, you are given a series of texts and an answer paper. You are allowed to use the texts to answer the questions, so you do not need to memorise them. You should refer to the texts closely while you are answering.

Achieving Level 3

The purpose of this book is to help you work towards and achieve Level 3.

Reading	
Level 2	At Level 2, you can read and understand simple texts. You can express opinions about major events or ideas in stories, poems and non-fiction. You can use phonics and grammar to read new words and work out what the text means.
Level 3	At Level 3, you can read different sorts of texts fluently and accurately. You can read without help and can work out what texts mean. You can understand the main points of fiction and non-fiction texts and can say which you prefer. You can use your knowledge of the alphabet to locate books and find information.

Writing	
Level 2	At Level 2, you can write both stories and information texts. You can choose words to interest the people who will read what you have written. You can write in sentences and you use capital letters and full stops. You can spell shorter words correctly and even if you make a mistake, it is easy to read. Your handwriting is neat and the letters are the right size.
Level 3	At Level 3, your writing is organised, imaginative and clear. You can use the main features of different forms of writing and you try to adapt to different readers. Your sentences follow each other logically and they are grammatically correct. You choose words for variety and interest. You can spell most high-frequency words correctly. You use full stops, capital letters and question marks accurately. Your handwriting is joined and legible.

Writing non-fiction

Non-fiction texts give you information about something or someone. They also give you facts and, sometimes, opinions.

Type of non-fiction	Definition and purpose	Where you might read an example
Recount	This tells you something that has already happened. It may include personal opinions and comments.	letters, diaries, newspapers, biographies and autobiographies
Instructions	These tell you how to do something step by step.	board games, recipes, directions, how to make or repair something
Non-chronological report	This gives you facts about a topic or a subject.	encyclopaedias, information books, posters, leaflets, travel guides
Explanation	This tells you how or why something happens or works.	leaflets, posters, manuals, letters, diagrams and information books
Persuasion	This tries to influence how you think about someone or something.	advertisements, articles, leaflets, spam emails
Discussion or balanced argument	This gives you information both for and against a topic.	newspaper articles, letters, magazines, information leaflets and posters

Survival tips

The tasks in the Non-fiction Writing Tests do not always tell you what text type you need to write. It often just says, 'Write an information text...'. So it is important that you think about what type of information text you are dealing with first.

Over to you!

1. Join Edgar the Explorer on the expedition to the jungle!
2. Work through each section and don't rush.
3. Make sure you understand the way it is organised and what the key language features are.
4. Have a go at the practice questions.

Handling the practice questions

Decide what the purpose of the writing is. This tells you which text type to write. The question might say, 'Write a letter describing a weekend away'. This tells you the text should be a RECOUNT. Or it might say, 'Write a letter to persuade someone to...'. This tells you to write PERSUASIVE text.

Decide who the audience is. This tells you what sort of language to include. The question might say, 'Write a letter to a friend...'. This tells you to use informal language because you know the audience well. Or it might say, 'Write a report for the local museum on...'. This tells you to use formal language because you don't know who will be reading it.

Once you have decided on the purpose and audience, plan, write and check your writing.

Where to get help

- ★ Pages 8–43 are designed to help you succeed in the Writing Test.
- ★ Pages 44–47 will help you to give 'voice' to your writing, sharpen up your punctuation and improve your grammar.
- ★ Pages 48–59 are practice tests to help you answer SATs-style questions.

Recount

Definition

A recount is a piece of writing that gives information about something that has happened in the past. A recount can include personal feelings and comments.

Purpose

To retell an event or events.

Text plan

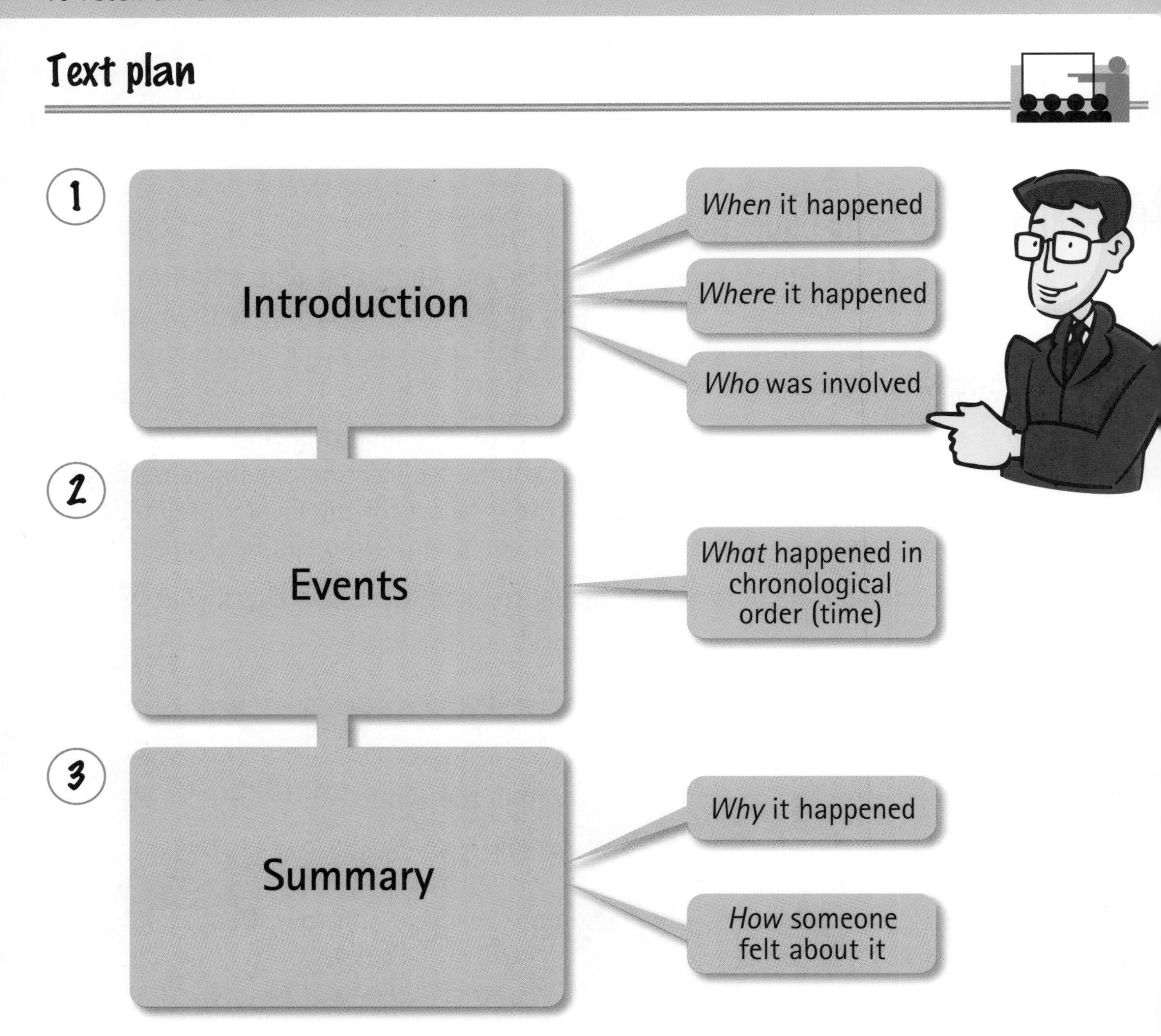

Look at the words in italics. You can use these as headings to help you plan a recount. Think about organising your recount into three paragraphs.

Language features

Events in a recount have already happened, so use verbs in the past tense:
e.g. '*We **found** the lost tribe*', **not** '*We **find** the lost tribe.*'

Use time connectives to link events:
e.g. ***First,*** *we arrived in the jungle.* ***Then,*** *we set up camp.*
Next, *we explored our surroundings.*

If you are in the recount, use the first person '*I*', '*we*', '*us*':
e.g. ***We*** *built a fire.*

If you are writing about someone else, use the third person '*he*', '*she*', '*they*':
e.g. ***They*** *reached the camp before us.*

Typical style

Recounts can be informal when you know the audience, e.g. a personal diary or a letter to a friend.

They can be formal when the audience is unknown, e.g. a newspaper article about a discovery, a biography or an autobiography of an explorer.

Find and list the time connectives in Edgar the Explorer's dairy on page 12. If you use a variety of connectives, you will get better marks.

Survival tips

Recounts can be in the form of a letter, a diary entry, biography, autobiography, newspaper article, sports report and news report. Remember to think about the purpose of the text.

Text example

Edgar the Explorer's diary

Wednesday July 1st

This morning we arrived at the campsite. At last! After such a long journey, I was so glad to be here.

First, all seven of our party had travelled by ship across the sea, then we trekked over desert by camel train and finally we paddled downriver in dug-out canoes.

We quickly put up our tents and soon the base camp was well organised. Matthew cooked a hot meal on an open fire and as we ate, we all listened to the strange sounds of the jungle in the humid night air. Later, I tucked into my blankets, settled on my camp bed and slept well, even though I was full of excitement.

My last thoughts were about finding a long-lost tribe, or even ancient treasures!

Practice questions

1. Imagine you are exploring with Edgar. Write your own personal diary entry about what happened on the day you arrived at the edge of the jungle.

   This is a short writing task. You have 20 minutes to plan, write and check your work.

2. Write a newspaper article about the long journey by the group of seven brave explorers. This is a long writing task, so you have 45 minutes to plan, write and check your work.

How did you do?

1 This task was to write your diary entry. Usually people keep diaries just for themselves, not for the whole world to read, so the audience was you. Did you use informal language and short sentences?

2 This task was to write a recount in the form of a newspaper article. The audience was the general public. This means that it should be a formal piece of writing with some interesting information. It should be written in the third person. You should have explained who the people in the article were because the readers would not know them. Did you use capital letters and full stops for all of your sentences? Did you use some paragraphs?

See page 60 for an example answer.

Instructions

Definition

Instructions tell a reader how to do or make something, or how to get somewhere.

Purpose

To instruct.

Text plan

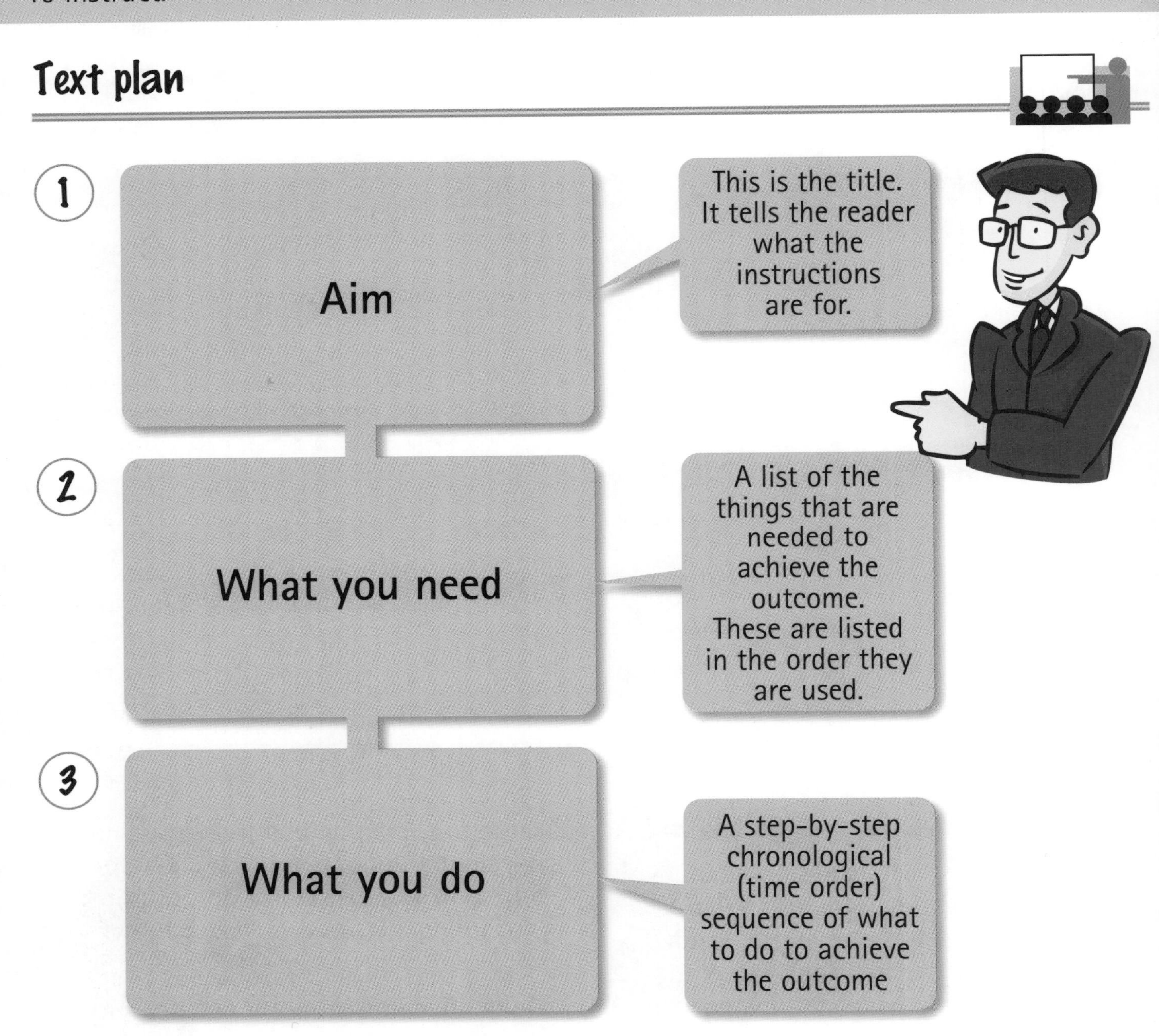

Usually in instructions you'll find a title and two headings. You need to decide on the best headings for the instructions you are writing. A recipe might have *Ingredients* and *Method* as headings. Directions could have just the title as you might not need anything else to achieve the outcome.

Language features

The 'What you need' section must have precise, accurate amounts, sizes and quantities,

e.g.: *6 rolls of film*
1 camera
1 tripod

Use time-based connectives, e.g. *'first'*, *'next'*, *'finally'*.

Use commands (the imperative voice):

e.g. ***Cross*** *the river below the rapids.*

Sometimes you might need to tell the reader how to carry out the instructions by using adverbs:

e.g. ***Slowly*** *creep forward.*

You can use numbers or bullet points to help the reader.

Typical style

Use short sentences. A reader doesn't want to wade through lots of words when they are following instructions.

Find and list the imperative verbs in the instructions on page 16.

Survival tips

Think 'step by step'. This will help you to write your instructions in the correct order.

Text example

How to make a cup of tea for seven explorers

What you need

★ a good camp fire
★ a metal tripod and hook
★ a billycan or pan
★ 1 litre of water
★ 7 tea bags
★ milk
★ 7 mugs
★ a teaspoon
★ sugar (optional)

1. Put a metal tripod and hook over the camp fire.
2. Build up the fire so it burns fiercely.
3. Fill a billycan or pan with fresh water.
4. Hang the can from the tripod hook.
5. Add wood to the fire until it is hot enough to boil the water.
6. Carefully remove the can from the tripod.
7. Place the tea bags in the water and stir.
8. Allow the tea to brew for one minute.
9. Pour the tea into the 7 mugs.
10. Add a little milk to each mug, stir with a spoon. Add sugar to taste.

Practice questions

1 Edgar is tired of eating the boring food that the campsite cook makes. Write some instructions to tell the cook how to prepare and cook your favourite meal.

This is a long writing task, so you have 45 minutes to plan, write and check your work.

2 Edgar has found holes in all of his socks! Write a set of instructions telling him how to mend them.

This is a short writing task. You have 20 minutes to plan, write and check your work.

How did you do?

1 This task was to write a set of instructions in the form of a recipe. The audience was the campsite cook. His usual cooking was described as boring, so he would need detailed information about the ingredients and clear steps that were easy to understand for the method. Did you use *Ingredients* and *Method* for your headings? Did you use *command* verbs at the beginning of each sentence?

2 This task was to write instructions on how to mend socks. The audience was Edgar. He might not be used to sewing. Did you list all the things he needed, e.g. wool, scissors, needle and thread? The instructions needed to be detailed, but you only had 20 minutes – no time to get carried away!

See pages 60–61 for an example answer.

Non-chronological report

Definition

Non-chronological reports give a reader information about something or somewhere. They are usually about a group of things, e.g. butterflies, not one thing in particular, e.g. Billy the butterfly. Facts about the subject are organised into paragraphs.

Purpose

To give information.

Text plan

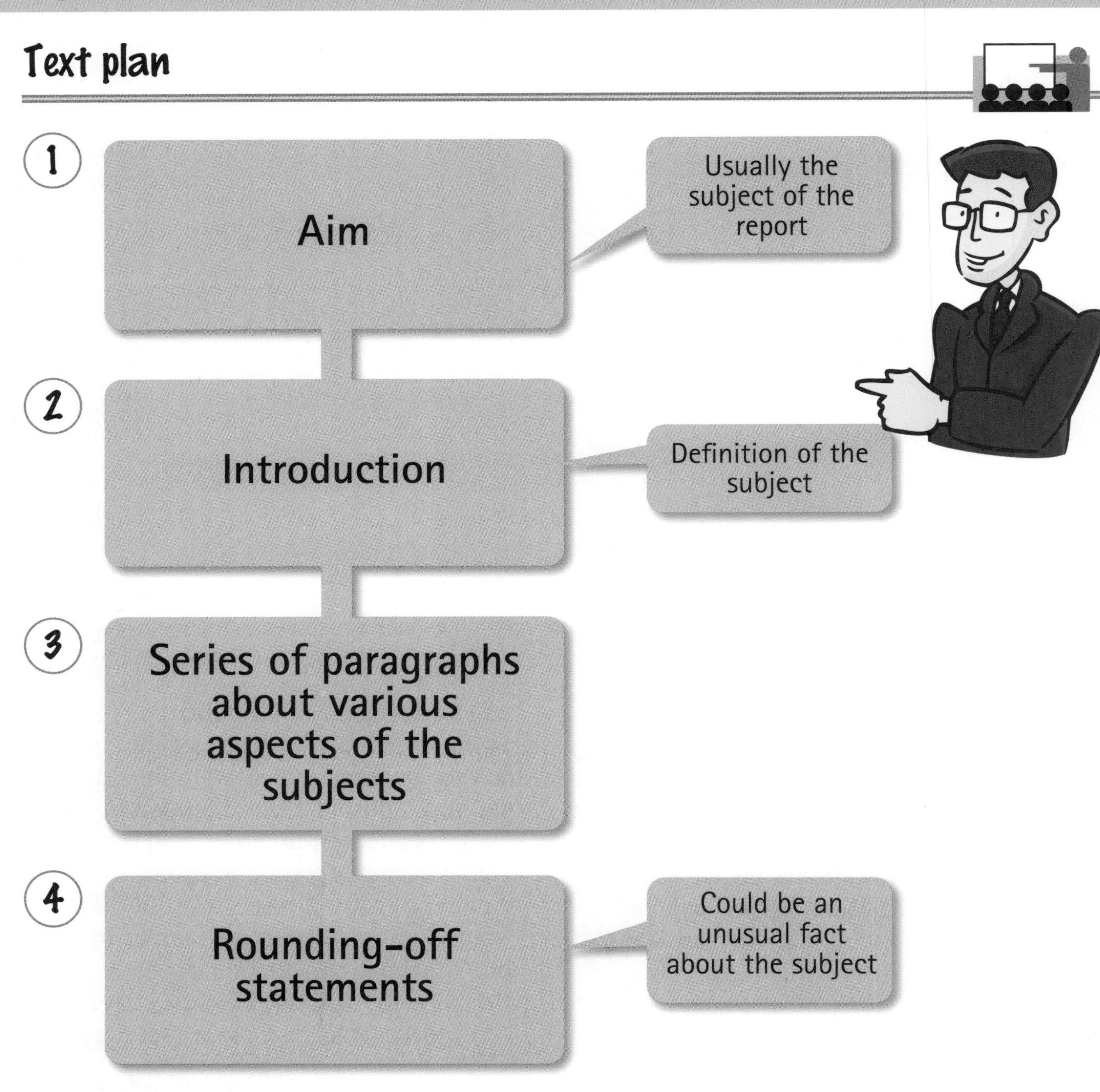

Language features

Use the PRESENT TENSE if the subject still exists:
e.g. *Many birds* ***live*** *in rainforests.*

Use the PAST TENSE if the subject does not still exist:
e.g. *Many dinosaurs* ***lived*** *in swamps.*

Use TECHNICAL VOCABULARY (specific language about the subject):
e.g. *Some dinosaurs were* ***herbivores****.*

Use factual ADJECTIVES to give more information:
e.g. *These birds have* ***red*** *and* ***black*** *tail feathers.*

Typical style

Use an IMPERSONAL voice. Don't give your opinions or say what you think. The purpose of your report is to give readers the facts.

Do not use imaginative language, e.g. *They have fluffy white feathers* ***like snowflakes in winter.*** Stick to the facts.

Think of a heading for each paragraph on page 20.
If you use paragraphs to organise your writing, you will get better marks.

Survival tips

Reports can be in the form of letters, encyclopaedia entries, information posters or leaflets as well as a straightforward piece of writing. A non-chronological report on a class of animals might include headings such as 'Appearance', 'Habitat' and 'Food'.

Text example

Jubbly-wubbly birds

Jubbly-wubbly birds are a newly-discovered species. They were discovered by Edgar the Explorer during an expedition to find the Lost Tribes of the jungle.

Jubbly-Wubbly birds are flightless birds and only found on the floor of the jungle. They are an important find for ornithologists because they have several unusual features never seen before.

They live in large flocks of about 20 birds and build nests in the centre of thick, thorny shrubs. A single flock of birds lives together in a community. They sleep together in the nest during the day and only emerge after sunset.

They travel as a group through the jungle to find food, which they take back to the nest and share with the flock. They eat seeds and nuts, but the main delicacy for Jubbly-wubbly birds is the rare, night-flowering Bango tree. This tree only flowers twice a year. Jubbly-wubbly flocks travel for several kilometres to find the flowers by following the tree's strong banana-like scent.

Jubbly-wubbly birds have large, heavy bodies. They are about one metre long from the beak to the tip of their tail feathers. Their beaks are hooked and adapted to break open the hard casing of nuts. However, they are also capable of picking up and carrying the Bango tree flower without crushing it. Jubbly-wubbly birds have large red feet with horny soles for walking on the jungle floor. Their plumage is green and brown.

Perhaps the most unusual feature of the Jubbly-wubbly bird is its song – a loud, harsh call: jubbly-wubby! jubbly-wubbly!

Practice questions

1. Edgar the Explorer has brought a new species of animal home to live in a jungle theme park. Write a leaflet to tell visitors about this new creature. You can choose what sort of creature it is, e.g. a bird, a reptile, an insect or a mammal.

   This is a long writing task, so you have 45 minutes to plan, write and check your work.

2. Write a short letter from Edgar to his wife describing what the jungle is like.

   This is a short writing task. You have 20 minutes to plan, write and check your work.

Survival tips

Decide what the AUDIENCE and PURPOSE is before you begin. This will help you choose the style and language features.

How did you do?

1. This task was to write a report in the form of a leaflet. The audience were the visitors to the jungle theme park. You did not know them, so you needed to write in a formal style. Did you introduce and define the animal first? Did you avoid describing too much about when and how it was discovered? Too much about the discovery might have turned the report into a recount. Did you describe facts using present tense verbs?

2. This task was to write a report in the form of a brief letter. The audience was Edgar's wife, so you could have used a friendly, chatty style with personal comments. But you should still have given factual information and sorted it logically. Did you group the facts into paragraphs? Did you remember to punctuate your writing correctly?

See page 61 for an example answer.

Explanation

Definition

An explanation tells the reader how or why something works or happens. It can be about natural things, e.g. why volcanoes erupt, or how a radio works.

Purpose

To explain.

Text plan

1. Title
2. Introduction
3. Paragraph describing the parts and/or appearance of the subject, or a process to be explained
4. Paragraph explaining why or how, often in time order
5. Concluding paragraph

Title: Tells the reader what the explanation is about. Often contains *how* or *why*.

Paragraph describing the parts and/or appearance: This defines the subject or process of the explanation.

Concluding paragraph: Summerising or rounding off. This could include where the subject or process occurs, or its effects.

Language features

Use PRESENT TENSE verbs if the subject is still around:
e.g. *When an insect **lands** on the lip of a pitcher plant, it **slips** down.*

Use PAST TENSE verbs if the subject existed in the past:
e.g. *Before digital cameras, photographers **used** rolls of film.*

Use TIME-BASED CONNECTIVES to show the order in which things happen:
e.g. *first, next, finally.*

Use CAUSE AND EFFECT CONNECTIVES to show how one thing makes something else happen or causes a result, e.g. *as, so that, in order to, because, this results in.*

Use TECHNICAL VOCABULARY (specific language for the subject):
e.g. *Bats use **echolocation** to avoid hitting obstacles.*

EXPLAIN technical words if you need to. You can define words in the text itself, or write a glossary, e.g. *echolocation: sound waves bouncing (echoing) off surfaces.*

Typical style

The PASSIVE VOICE, e.g. *Bats are found...* This can make the explanation more formal, but don't overdo it. Remember to use a variety of sentence types.

Find and list the connective words and phrases in the explanation on page 24. Group them by time or cause and effect. If you use a variety of connectives, you will get better marks.

Survival tips

Explanations can be in the form of letters, diagrams, information leaflets, encyclopedia entries and posters.

Text example

How pitcher plants feed

Today, I found a most unusual plant. It is shaped like a jug or pitcher, so I am naming it the pitcher plant.

This plant is found all over the jungle. It has a flower that hangs like a cup, or a pitcher, and is filled with liquid. This liquid is the plant's digestive juice.

First, insects are attracted to the plant and land on the rim of the flower because it has bright colours and a strong scent. This rim is slippery, which causes the insect to slide down the smooth sides of the flower into the digestive juices. The insect is now trapped and drowns in the fluid. The digestive juices slowly dissolve the insect and it is absorbed by the plant as food.

This is a wonderful discovery, and I can't wait to find more amazing plants and animals here in this jungle.

Practice questions

1 You have invented a special container to help explorers carry their plant and insect specimens when they leave the jungle and return home. Write a letter to the leader of an expedition to explain how to use it.

This is a long writing task, so you have 45 minutes to plan, write and check your work.

2 Five members of the expedition need to row across a river to find some fruit to eat but none of them understand how a rowing boat works. Write a note telling them how it works.

This is a short writing task. You have 20 minutes to plan, write and check your work.

How did you do?

1 This task was to write an explanation in the form of a letter. The audience was an important explorer. This means that the letter and explanation should be formal in style. Check that you have written the letter using present tense verbs.

- If you have used past tense verbs, then it has turned into a recount.
- If you wrote telling the explorer how to work the system himself, then it has turned into instructions.

2 This task was to write an explanation for your own expedition members. This means that you know them fairly well, so the tone can be quite informal. Did you remember to write an explanation, and not a set of instructions? The explanation should be clear and concise to help the crew members to understand it. Did you sequence your explanation using time-based and cause-and-effect connectives?

See page 61 for an example answer.

Persuasion

Definition

A persuasive text tries to make the reader think, do or buy something.

Purpose

To persuade.

Text plan

1. **The main point of the text** — Could be a statement or a question. Grab the reader's attention!

2. **Supporting points** — Organise your supporting points into paragraphs.

3. **Summary of key reasons** — Repeat the key points to reinforce them.

4. **Call to action** — Ask the reader to take action, e.g. to buy something, to think something, to go somewhere.

Language features

Usually PRESENT TENSE but could move into the past or the future, depending on the point being made.

Support each point with EVIDENCE. This could be numbers or statistics, facts or opinions and quotes.

Appeal to your readers by using EMOTIVE LANGUAGE, e.g:

- *This **appalling** situation ...*
- *This will **delight** and **enchant** all children.*

Ask a RHETORICAL QUESTION to involve your reader to get them on your side and agree with your point, e.g. a question to which you already know the answer, or ask a question and give the answer.

- *Would you like to have **excitement** and **adventure**?*
- *Do you want to be a **famous** explorer?*
- *Who pays for all this **waste**? You do!*

Use LOGICAL CONNECTIVES to reason with the reader:
e.g. *therefore, consequently, furthermore, so, thus.*

Typical style

Use the PASSIVE VOICE if you don't want to say where your evidence comes from, e.g. *It is believed ..., many people think ...*

How many passive verb-phrases can you find in the text on page 28? If you can use one or two passive verbs, you will get better marks.

Survival tips

Persuasive texts can be written in many forms. They can be letters, posters, leaflets, advertisements, newspaper and magazine articles.

Remember to think about the *purpose* of the text, which is to persuade, and the *audience*, the people you want to persuade.

Text example

Dear Mr Roberts,

Would you like to involve your pupils in an exciting, educational opportunity that's not to be missed?

My name is Edgar the Explorer and I am writing to invite you to send some of your pupils on the trip of a lifetime.

Many people believe that today's children are denied the chances we had in our youth: to explore, to challenge themselves, to develop individual personalities. In short – they are becoming couch potatoes only interested in television and computer games.

I believe the solution has been found!

I am putting together a children's expedition to the jungle. All the children who join will encounter sights, sounds and experiences that will be the envy of their friends. In addition, they will develop independence and self-reliance. Furthermore, their knowledge of the world and its inhabitants will be improved enormously.

The children will be taken by ship over the sea to the jungle, where they will enjoy trekking, canoeing and camping.

All this can be secured with a deposit of £50 per child, followed by a very reasonable charge of £500.

Do you want to ensure a better future for your pupils? I am sure a wise and enlightened teacher such as you will want to grasp this opportunity.

Please reply as soon as you can.

Yours sincerely,

Edgar the Explorer

Practice questions

1. You are really keen to join Edgar the Explorer on the children's expedition. Unfortunately, you cannot afford the cost of the trip. Write a letter to Edgar to persuade him to take you for free.

   This is a long writing task, so you have 45 minutes to plan, write and check your work.

2. Your school is holding a jungle-themed fundraising event. Write an advert for the event to persuade people to come along.

   This is a short writing task. You have 20 minutes to plan, write and check your work.

Survival tips

Think in *threes*! You could make three points, give three reasons, or use three statements to summarise. Think about *repetition*. Reinforce your main point by repeating it using different words.

If you can, use some emotive vocabulary and appeal to the reader's point of view. You will get better marks.

How did you do?

1. This task was to write a persuasive text in the form of a letter. The audience was the leader of the expedition and therefore an important person. This means that it should be quite a formal piece of writing. You need to have thought carefully about how to appeal to Edgar and supported your points with evidence and reasons. Did you reinforce your main point? Did you summarise your points in the conclusion? Did you organise your letter into paragraphs? Did you use correct punctuation?

2. This task was to write a persuasive text in the form of an advert. The audience was the local public. This means it should be fairly formal and give key information, e.g. what the event is, when and where it takes place and what the attractions are. Did you give the key information using brief language? Did you attract the readers' attention?

See pages 61–62 for an example answer.

Discussion

Definition

A discussion text is sometimes called a *balanced argument*. This gives the reader information about an issue from different points of view. Readers are left to make up their own mind about how they feel about the issue.

Purpose

To present opposing points of view about an issue.

Text plan

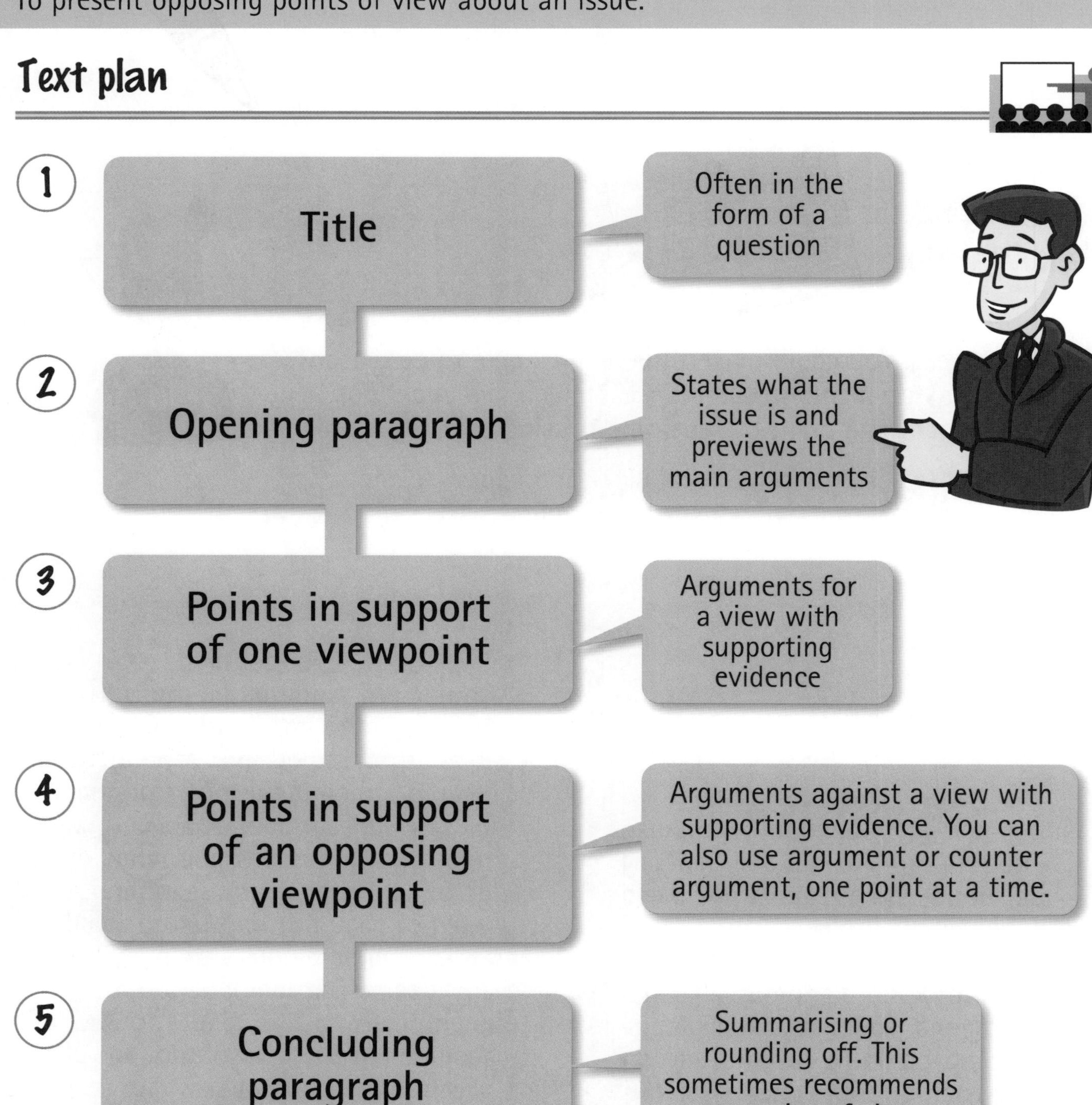

Language features

You can use PRESENT TENSE verbs or the PAST TENSE depending on the issue.

Use LOGICAL CONNECTIVES to help you organise your argument:
e.g. *therefore, consequently, so.*

Use connectives that show the OPPOSITE view:
e.g. *but, however, nevertheless.*

Use a CONNECTIVE in the final paragraph to signal that you are SUMMING UP,
e.g. *in conclusion, to summarise, finally.*

Use EVIDENCE and EXAMPLES to support the points made about the issue. These could be numbers and statistics, facts or quotes.

Typical style

Use an IMPERSONAL STYLE. Say what PEOPLE think, not what you think.

Use the PASSIVE VOICE, particularly when you don't want to say where you get your evidence from:
e.g. *It is thought that..., it is believed...*

Find and list the connectives in the discussion on page 32. If you use a variety of connectives, you will get better marks.

Survival tips

Arguments can be in the form of information leaflets, newspaper and magazine articles. Remember to support your ideas with evidence.

Text example

Should we search for the Lost Tribes of the jungle?

An open letter to the Committee for Exploring Everywhere (C.E.E.)

An expedition has been planned to go in search of the Lost Tribes of the jungle.

Although these tribes have never been found, there is evidence that they do exist. The recent expedition, lead by Edgar the Explorer, returned with pictures of footprints, samples of cooking utensils and primitive weapons. Until now, the tribes have survived in the jungle without any interference from the outside world.

Many people argue that an essential part of progress is the knowledge of all places and peoples in the world. They believe we can improve the lives of these people through education. They also think we can learn about our history and evolution from the discovery of these Lost Tribes.

However, others think they should be left alone. These people have survived without our help, so why should we interfere? Also, they question the wisdom of exposing the Lost Tribes to the germs and viruses that, so far, have never affected them. A spokesperson for LOLTA (Leave Our Lost Tribes Alone) recently said he feared our interference would threaten their very survival.

In conclusion, there are many points of view surrounding this issue which need careful consideration by the C.E.E. before a final decision is made.

Practice questions

1. Edgar the Explorer and his expedition are in trouble! Edgar has lost the map. Some of the party think they should turn back before they get lost. Others think they should carry on without the map. Your task is to write both sides of the argument clearly so you can deliver a speech before they hold a final vote.

   This is a long writing task, so you have 45 minutes to plan, write and check your work.

2. There is to be a parliamentary debate on 'what to do about the Lost Tribes of the jungle'. Write a summary using bullet points to help a speaker set the scene for the debate. Use the discussion text on page 32 to help you.

   This is a short writing task. You have 20 minutes to plan, write and check your work.

How did you do?

1. This task was to write an argument as a speech to your fellow explorers. This means that you know your audience well, so the tone could be informal. However, the debate is important to them, so you should have organised your points clearly in paragraphs. You should also have followed the typical structure of an argument.

2. This task was to write an argument in bullet point form to summarise the issue and provide someone with notes about it. You needed to identify the issue, and write your points briefly, but you still needed to give supporting evidence. See page 62 for an example answer.

Writing fiction

Fiction texts can be in the form of stories, poems or plays. In this section, we are concentrating on writing stories. Their purpose is to entertain readers and to appeal to their emotions. They can make readers sad, happy or frightened.

There are four things all stories have in common:

structure setting characters theme

Where to get help

★ Pages 35–36 look at story structure and story ingredients.

★ Pages 37–42 look at each ingredient in more detail. Each section gives you hints, tips ideas and examples. There are also some practice questions for short writing tasks.

★ Page 43 looks at planning stories. Planning is important so don't skip this bit!

Survival tips

Keep a 'Writing Ideas' book. All writers 'borrow' ideas from other writers. So, read! Note down good ideas, words and phrases that you like. Use them in your own writing.

Your reader doesn't know what was inside your head when you wrote. So make sure you tell or show them. If your character moves from the house to the park, tell the reader the setting has changed.

Use paragraphs. Think Person, Time, Place (PTP). When the person, the time or the place changes in your story, start a new paragraph.

Over to you!

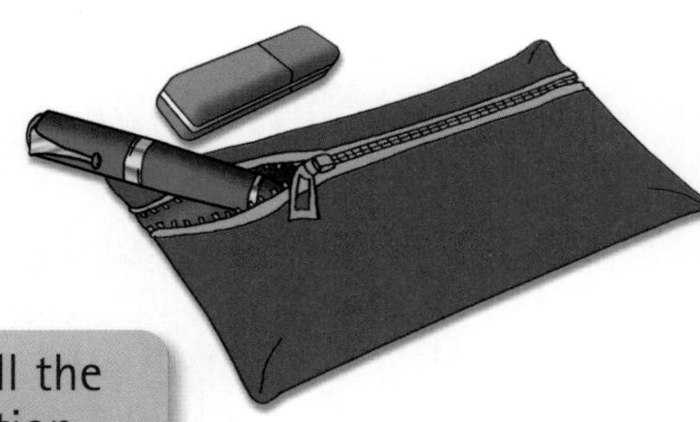

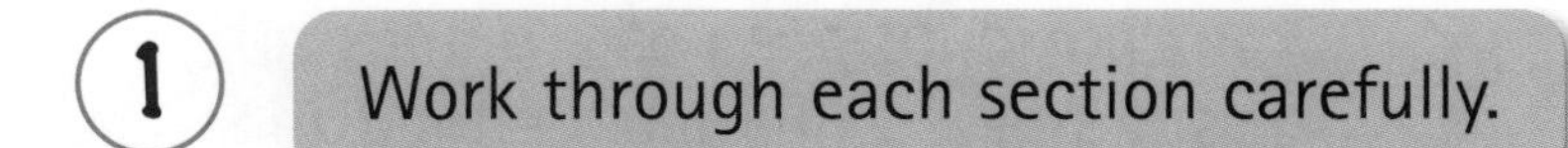

1. Work through each section carefully.

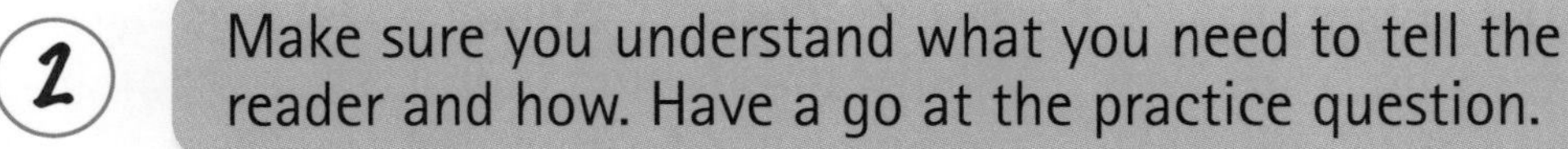

2. Make sure you understand what you need to tell the reader and how. Have a go at the practice question.

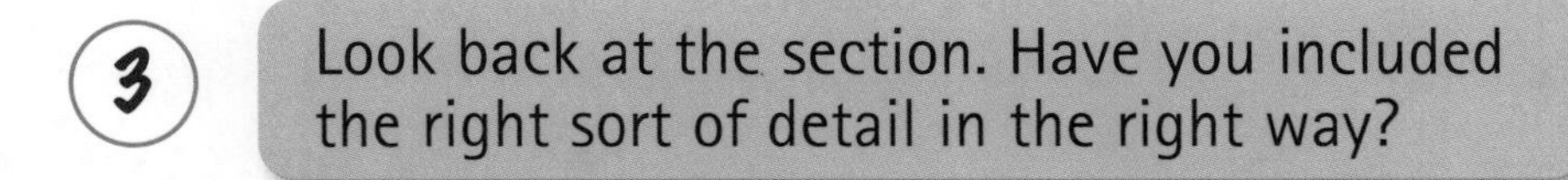

3. Look back at the section. Have you included the right sort of detail in the right way?

Story structure

All stories are organised in the same basic way. When you plan your story, think in five sections.

Beginning

Introduce the setting and the main characters.

Build-up

The story gets going. Something happens.

Problem

Something goes wrong! This is the most exciting part of the story.

Resolution

The problem gets sorted out.

Ending

All the loose ends are tied up. The characters think or reflect on what has happened.

Setting, characters and theme

Before planning your story, you need to decide on the main ingredients.

Setting

This is WHEN and WHERE your story takes place. You need to help your readers make a picture in their minds. The setting can also be used to create an atmosphere, which can affect how the reader feels.

Characters

This is WHO is in the story. You need to help the readers build up a picture of the characters – not just APPEARANCE but also PERSONALITY.

Think about some stories you have read. Who were the characters? What were they like? How do you know? What were they called? Look at some short stories to help you.

Theme

This is WHAT happens in the story. Some people say that there are only a few themes in the world. All writers borrow ideas from other stories and this is something you can do.

Think about stories you have read. What happened? Did one story remind you of any others? Think about some common themes, e.g. good overcomes evil, main character loses something.

Setting

Introduce the setting at the beginning of the story. Remember the two things you need to tell your reader are WHEN and WHERE the story is set.

When and where?

The big picture

Is your story set in the past, the present (now) or the future? Look at these three examples. How have the writers told the reader about the big picture?

- The spacecraft slowly descended to the surface of the planet.
- Captain Edgar stuffed his spyglass through his belt, straightened his tricorn hat and began to stride across the quarterdeck.
- Jon eagerly put his new Jungle Adventure DVD into the player and pressed play.

Above, the writers have used objects to tell us WHEN and WHERE the stories are set. Spacecraft and planets point to this story being set in the future. A spyglass, tricorn hat and quarterdeck tell us the next story is probably set in the past. The DVD shows us that this final story is set in the present day.

The smaller picture

Writers tell us more about the setting by adding smaller details. Look how these writers tell us about the season in which their stories are set.

- Jon settled down to enjoy the next hour and ignored the rain and wind as they lashed the last of the leaves from the trees outside.
- Edgar shielded his eyes as the snowflakes grew thicker and peered into the murky distance.

These are more interesting ways than just saying, '*It was a cold winter's day*', or '*On a wet autumn afternoon*'. Remember, if you set your story in the future in space, there is no weather.

The even smaller picture

At what time of day is your story happening? How can you tell the reader without being too obvious? Look how these writers have done it.

- ★ They watched as the sun slowly rose above the horizon of the purple planet; a new day began that would last five Earth-years long.
- ★ The Moon glinted on the lapping waves as the rowing boat was pushed off the side.
- ★ 'Supper's ready, Jon,' called mum from the kitchen.

Get involved!

You need to involve your reader and help them experience the setting inside their head. This is where you can start to use the five senses:

sight **sound** **touch** **smell** **taste**

Don't overdo it, though! All the senses at once will overwhelm the reader. Make it a rule to use no more than three senses at one time.

Can you spot which three senses the writer has used in this paragraph?

> The wooden planks of the deck were warm under Ben's bare feet as he crept across the deck. He eagerly breathed in the salty air after the musty stench below decks, and blinked as the bright sunlight hit his eyes.

Survival tips

If you are writing a short task that asks you to describe a setting, you can afford to put in lots of details. In a long writing task, where the setting is just one of the story ingredients, you need to introduce the setting briefly. You can add more detail during the plot.

Text example

Setting description

The harsh cries of strange birds filled the air as they swooped and wheeled around the cove where *HMS Intrepid* lay moored. Edgar eagerly gripped the sun-warmed railing as he stood on deck and looked across the rough breakers crashing on the shore at the edge of a forest. The long journey was now forgotten and the real adventure beckoned.

Read the setting description and answer these questions:

★ What time of day is it?
★ What sounds does Edgar hear?
★ What does Edgar see?
★ What does Edgar touch?

Practice questions

Write a setting description for one of the following places:

1 A ship at sea
2 Your bedroom
3 A desert island
4 A busy shopping centre

This is a short writing task. You have 20 minutes to plan, write and check your work.

Characters

Introduce your main characters at the beginning of the story. Have a picture of your characters in your mind. Three things to make your character 'real' are:

- ★ what they look like
- ★ what they say and how they say it
- ★ how they move.

What they look like

You can describe the character's face, hair and clothes. What do you think this character is like?

> Smoothly and easily, he sprang out of the jeep. His tanned young face stood out against his sun-bleached hair.

What they say

Dialogue adds variety to your writing. But dialogue needs to move the story along.

> 'What are you doing?' he yelled angrily. He came towards us, fists clenched.

The writer has added dialogue telling us what the characters said, but also how they said it by using powerful speech-verbs and adverbs. There is also more about movement.

This description tells us something about the character's appearance. What else has the writer told us about this character?
Look for clues in the descriptions. Think about these things.

- ★ Appearance – why do they look the way they do?
- ★ Dialogue – what does the dialogue tell you about the person's feelings and personality?
- ★ Movement – what does the way they move tell you about the character?

Survival tips

- Names can tell readers a lot about a character, e.g. what do you think *Dilys Dumpling* might be like? Try to make the names suit the character.
- Keep to two or three characters only. If you have two characters, make one male and one female, then there is no confusion about pronouns ('*he*' or '*she*').
- Only use dialogue when it tells the reader more about the character or the plot. Don't waste words on idle chit-chat.
- Don't tell your reader everything. Give clues by how they speak and move.
- Voice! If you are telling the story using the first person '*I*' or '*We*', stick to it. If you use a third person narrator, remember to use '*he*', '*she*' or '*they*'.

Practice questions

Choose one of these topics to write about.

This is a short writing task. You have 20 minutes to plan, write and check your work.

1. Old Tom runs a jungle playground. One day, he sees two boys bullying a younger boy. Write a story opening to describe the setting and characters.

2. A new girl joins your class at school and you think she could be a friend. Write a story opening to describe the setting and characters.

Themes

Most stories have simple themes – good beats bad, lost and found, wishing.

Explore

Which themes do you think belong to these well-known stories?

A. The Lord of the Rings

B. Harry Potter

C. Cinderella

Basic structure

Good overcomes evil

Beginning	Two characters – one good one evil. The setting is established.
Build-up	Evil character plots against the good character. Good character is innocently unaware.
Problem	Evil character tricks or threatens to harm the good character.
Resolution	The good character outwits the evil character.
Ending	Everything is okay. The characters reflect or think about what has happened.

Planning

Planning is an extremely useful way of thinking about story ingredients and organising your ideas. In the SATs long writing task, you have only about 10 minutes planning time. That's not very long at all!

So, you need to work out a way of planning that is fast and works for you. Try using the story organiser below.

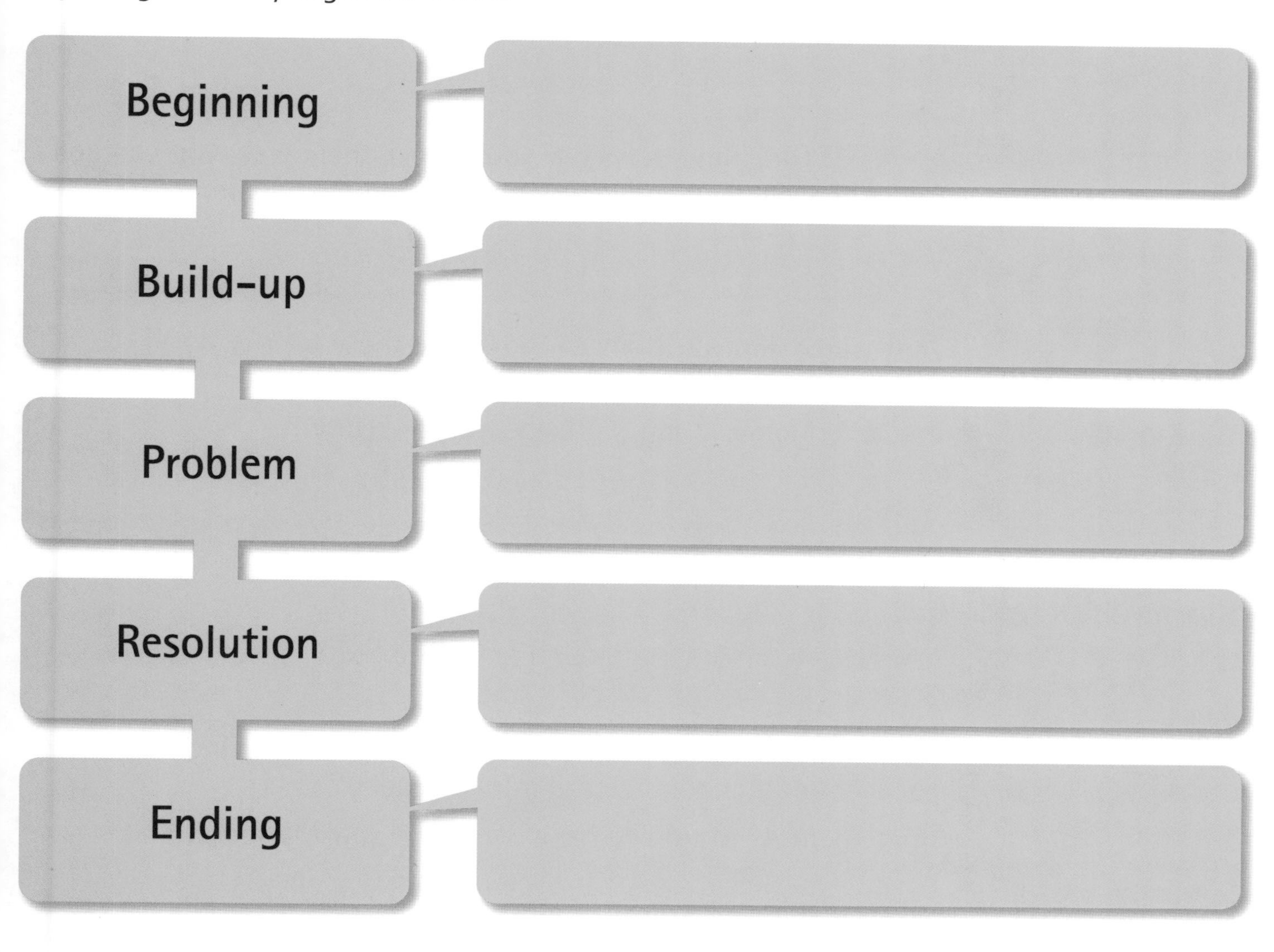

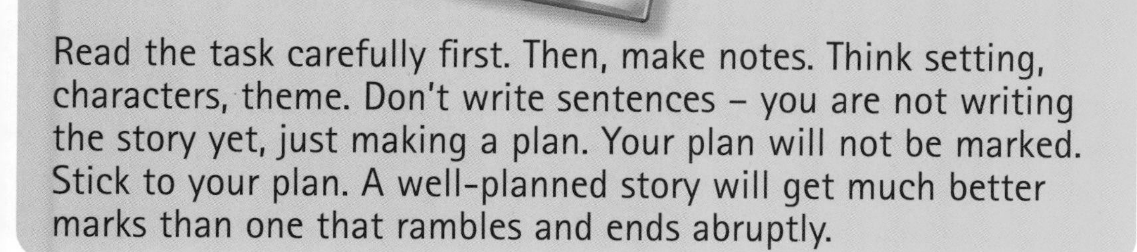

Survival tips

Read the task carefully first. Then, make notes. Think setting, characters, theme. Don't write sentences – you are not writing the story yet, just making a plan. Your plan will not be marked. Stick to your plan. A well-planned story will get much better marks than one that rambles and ends abruptly.

Grammar

The next step is to polish up your grammar. It could make the final difference to your writing.

In a Level 3 piece of writing, the writer needs to:

- ★ use different types of SENTENCES and PUNCTUATE them correctly
- ★ organise writing into PARAGRAPHS or SECTIONS
- ★ use CONNECTIVES such as *'and'*, *'but'*, *'so'*, *'when'*.

Vocabulary

You need to think about ADJECTIVES and VERBS. If you choose them well, you can get better marks. Try not to use the same adjective or verb over and over again.

What words can you think of to replace these overused adjectives and verbs?

good big nice very really

put got went said

Sentences

Use a variety of sentence types – simple, compound and complex.

Simple sentences

These are easy to write and read. They have one clause: It was raining. Using a lot of simple sentences one after another can be boring for a reader.

Edgar went out. It was raining hard. He crossed the clearing. He saw the snake.

Compound sentences

These have two or more clauses that are as important as each other. They can be joined by these connectives – *'and'*, *'but'*, *'so'*, *'like'*.

It was raining hard, so Edgar put up his brolly.

Complex sentences

If you use complex sentences as well as simple and compound ones, you have a very good chance of achieving Level 4. Complex sentences always have a clause or clauses that are less important than the other clauses.

Edgar was keen to photograph the snake, although it was raining so hard that the camera was soaking wet.

Connectives

Remember, you should use a variety of suitable connectives in your writing. Connectives are words and phrases that link clauses.

There are different connectives for different purposes. If you look back at the non-fiction section on pages 8–33, the types of connective that you can use for different text types are listed.

When you are writing stories, you usually use time-based connectives. Look at these suggestions for different types of connectives.

What we often write	What you can use instead	
Addition AND or AND THEN	furthermore moreover also	
Against BUT	on the other hand nevertheless however	
Time THEN or AND THEN	meanwhile afterwards once later next	just then all at once suddenly when finally
Cause and effect BECAUSE	this means that this leads to as as result so that as	this results in consequently in order to so
Logical BECAUSE or SO	therefore consequently	furthermore thus
Summing up FINALLY	in conclusion to summarise as a result	

Survival tips

- ★ Don't use the same connective over and over again in one piece of writing.
- ★ Make a connectives list and learn the words.
- ★ Collect new connectives from your reading.

Punctuation

Punctuation tells your reader how to read your writing. Correct punctuation makes sense of your writing and stops your reader from getting confused.

A Level 3 piece of writing needs accurate use of FULL STOPS, CAPITAL LETTERS, EXCLAMATION MARKS and QUESTION MARKS. You should always remember to use COMMAS in a list.

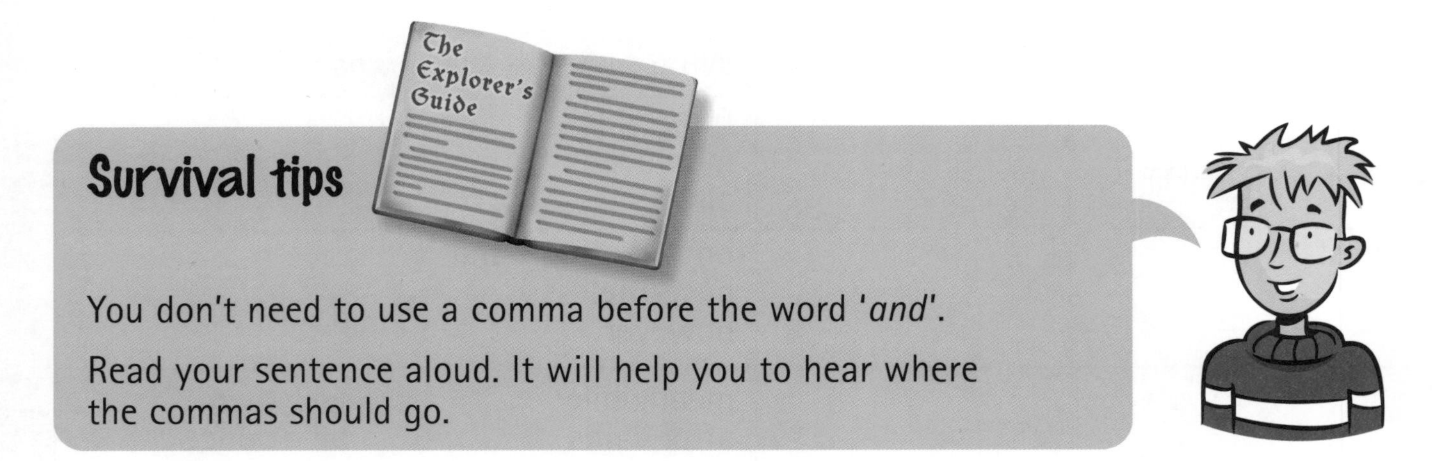

Survival tips

You don't need to use a comma before the word '*and*'.

Read your sentence aloud. It will help you to hear where the commas should go.

Speech

There are two ways of telling a reader what a character says.

Indirect speech

This is also known as 'reported' speech. It's when you don't use the speaker's exact words but report what was said.

The captain said they would be arriving soon.

Edgar threatened to close the camp if conditions did not improve.

Direct speech

You can use the speaker's actual words inside speech marks (' ') but there is a bit more punctuation needed. The most common punctuation is a comma.

"We are going to discover wonderful and new species," he declared.

Here, the comma is used at the end of the spoken words INSIDE the speech marks.

If the speaker continues speaking the same sentence, you need another comma before the next spoken words.

"We are going to discover wonderful and new species," he declared,
"and then we will all be rich!"

Apostrophes

Take special care with apostrophes. They can change the meaning of a sentence when used badly.

There are only two reasons to use an apostrophe:

★ to show that something belongs to somebody (possession)
★ to show that a letter or letters have been missed out (omission).

Possession

The captain's cabin – this shows that the cabin belonged to the captain.

Be careful if the noun is a plural noun, i.e. more than one.

The ship's crew – this means the crew belonging to one ship.
The ships' crews – this means all the crews belonging to all the ships.

Omission

Sometimes a letter or part of a word is missed out to make a shortened form. This often occurs in direct speech so that it sounds natural.

could not becomes *couldn't*
was not becomes *wasn't*
captain can become *cap'n*

Survival tips

The word '*it*' – this is the really tricky one. Learn the rule and you won't make mistakes!

- The apostrophe is ONLY EVER used with the word '*it*' when a letter is missed out (the shortened form).
  '*It is a great adventure*' becomes '*It's a great adventure*'.
- The apostrophe is NEVER EVER used to show possession with '*it*'.
  Look at that bird. Its wings are enormous.
- NEVER EVER use an apostrophe with plural nouns UNLESS it shows possession.

Reading comprehension

About the Reading Test

The Reading Test comes in the form of two booklets – one containing the texts you will read, and another for your answers. You have 45 minutes to read the booklets and answer all the questions.

Reading the texts

Read the texts in the booklet. DON'T RUSH. Try to immerse yourself in the story or information and enjoy it. When you have finished, take a moment to reflect and think about what you have read. Did it make sense? Was there anything you didn't understand?

Answering the questions

Read the instructions before you begin. Read them carefully as they give you information about how to answer the questions.

Now you can begin to answer the questions. Remember to REFER TO THE TEXT. You do not need to answer any questions from memory.

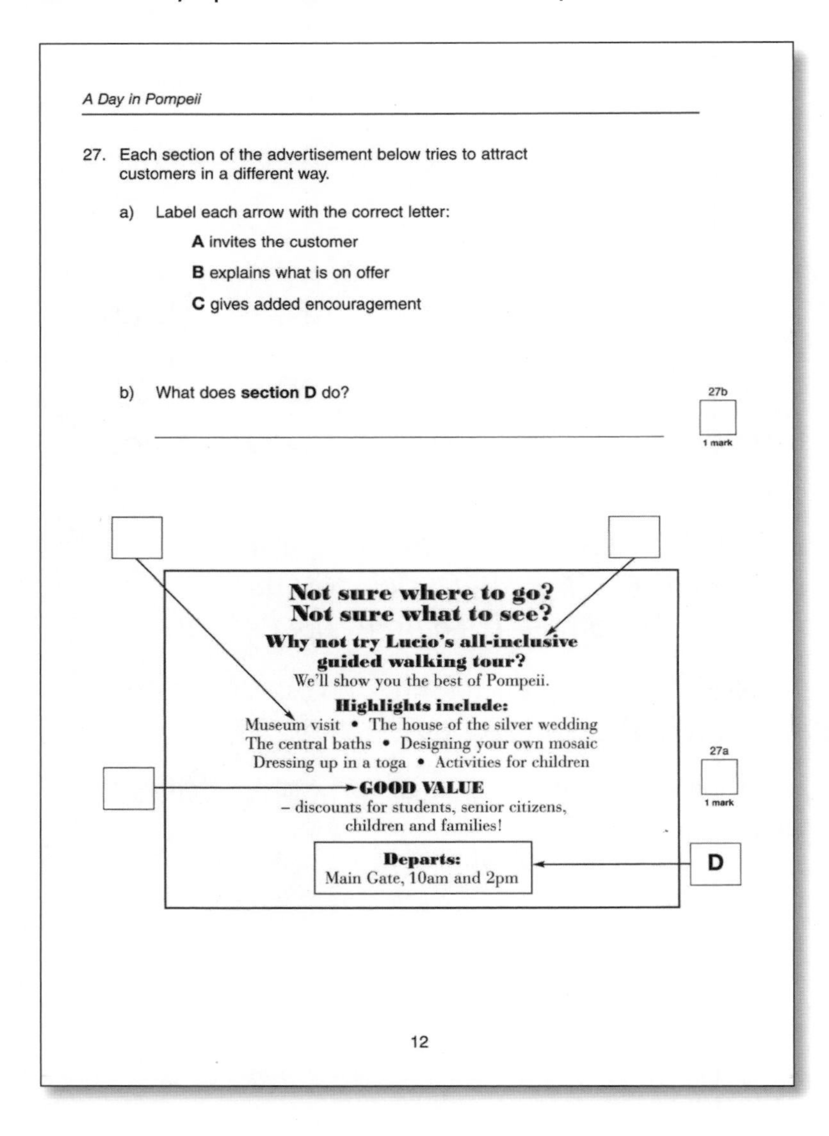

A Day in Pompeii

27. Each section of the advertisement below tries to attract customers in a different way.

    a) Label each arrow with the correct letter:

    A invites the customer

    B explains what is on offer

    C gives added encouragement

    b) What does **section D** do?

    27b — 1 mark

Not sure where to go?
Not sure what to see?
Why not try Lucio's all-inclusive guided walking tour?
We'll show you the best of Pompeii.
Highlights include:
Museum visit • The house of the silver wedding
The central baths • Designing your own mosaic
Dressing up in a toga • Activities for children
GOOD VALUE
– discounts for students, senior citizens, children and families!
Departs:
Main Gate, 10am and 2pm

D

27a — 1 mark

12

The questions

Always read the question carefully before you begin to write. Then you will understand what you are being asked to do.

The questions are there to test that you can:

- ★ make sense of what you are reading
- ★ find information and ideas in the text
- ★ work out what the author meant
- ★ understand why a text is organised in a particular way
- ★ comment on vocabulary and style
- ★ say how a text makes you feel
- ★ link what you read to your own life.

Survival tips

- ★ Check how many marks each question is worth.
- ★ One mark usually means the answer is in the WORDS of the text.
- ★ Two marks or three marks usually means that you are asked to work out what the author meant. You are meant to read between the lines, or draw on your own knowledge and experience.
- ★ Always answer two- or three-mark questions with evidence or examples from the text.
- ★ When a question begins, 'Why do you think...?' or 'How do you know...?', you should always BACK UP YOUR ANSWER with examples from the text.

The Wind Singer

William Nicholson

Long ago...

At the time the strangers came, the Manth people were still living in the low mat-walled shelters that they had carried with them in their hunting days. The domed huts were clustered around the salt mine that was to become the source of their wealth. This was long before they had built the great city that stands above the salt caverns today.
One high summer afternoon, a band of travellers came striding out of the desert plains, and made camp nearby. They wore their hair long and loose, men and women alike, and moved slowly and spoke quietly, when they spoke at all. They traded a little with the Manth, buying bread and meat and salt, paying with small silver ornaments that they themselves had made. They caused no trouble, but their near presence was somehow uncomfortable. Who were they? Where had they come from? Where were they going? Direct questions produced no answers: only a smile, a shrug, a shake of the head.

Then the strangers were seen to be at work, building a tower. Slowly a wooden structure took shape, a platform higher than a man, on which they constructed a second narrower tower, out of timber beams and metal pipes. These pipes were all of different sizes, and bundled together, like the pipes of an organ. At their base, they opened out into a ring of metal horns. At their upper end, they funnelled together to form a single cylinder, like a neck, and then fanned out again to end in a ring of large leather scoops. When the wind blew, the scoops caught it and the entire upper structure rotated, swinging round to face the strongest gusts. The swirling air was funnelled through the neck to the ranked pipes, to emerge from the horns as a series of meaningless sounds.

The tower had no obvious purpose of any kind. For a while it was a curiosity, and the people would stare at it as it creaked this way and that. When the wind blew hard, it made a mournful moaning that was comical at first, but soon became tiresome.

Questions

These questions are about the beginning of the novel *The Wind Singer* by William Nicholson.

1 Circle your answer. Long ago the Manth people lived in ... (*1 mark*)

domed huts **caravans** **tents**

2 What time of year was it when the strangers came? (*1 mark*)

3 How did the strangers pay for goods they bought from the Manth people? (*1 mark*)

4 How does the author tell you this part of the novel is a flashback? (*2 marks*)

5 Why do you think the Manth people felt uncomfortable with the strangers? (*3 marks*)

6 What was the purpose of the leather scoops? (*3 marks*)

Find the words in the text.

Read between the lines.

Think about what happens to the tower. Write a sentence giving evidence from the text.

Great Expectations

Charles Dickens

Chapter 2

Joe's forge adjoined our house, which was a wooden house, as many of the dwellings in our country were – most of them, at that time. When I ran home from the churchyard, the forge was shut up, and Joe was sitting alone in the kitchen. Joe and I being fellow sufferers, and having confidences as such, Joe imparted a confidence to me, the moment I raised the latch of the door and peeped in at him opposite to it, sitting in the chimney corner.

'Mrs Joe has been out a dozen times, looking for you, Pip. And she's out now, making it a baker's dozen.'

'Is she?'

'Yes, Pip,' said Joe, 'and what's worse, she's got Tickler with her.' At this dismal intelligence, I twisted the only button on my waistcoat round and round, and looked in great depression at the fire. Tickler was a wax-ended piece of cane, worn smooth by collision with my tickled frame.

'She sat down,' said Joe, 'and she got up, and she made a grab at Tickler, and she rampaged out. That's what she did,' said Joe, slowly clearing the fire between the lower bars with the poker, and looking at it: 'she rampaged out, Pip.'

'Has she been gone long, Joe?' I always treated him as a larger species of child, and as no more than my equal.

'Well,' said Joe, glancing up at the Dutch clock, 'she's been on the rampage, this last spell, about five minutes, Pip. She's a-coming! Get behind the door, old chap, and have the jack-towel betwixt you.'

Questions

These questions are about *Great Expectations* by Charles Dickens. This novel was written more than a hundred years ago. Pip lives with his sister, Mrs Joe Gargery and her husband, a blacksmith.

1. Where had Pip been before he went home? (*1 mark*)

2. What was joined onto the house? (*1 mark*)

3. Who was sitting in the chimney corner? (*1 mark*)

4. What does the phrase 'fellow sufferers' tell you about Pip and Joe? (*3 marks*)

5. Why does 'Tickler' begin with a capital letter? (*2 marks*)

6. Why does Pip look at the fire 'in great depression'? (*3 marks*)

Great explorers – a biography

Sir John Franklin (1786–1847)

Sir John Franklin was an Arctic explorer. He surveyed and made maps of the Arctic Ocean and the coast of Canada. He was also an officer in the Royal Navy and took part in a famous sea battle – the battle of Trafalgar. He is remembered most of all for his expeditions to find the North-West Passage, a sea route across the continent of North America.

Early life

Franklin was born on April 16th, 1786, in Spilsby, Lincolnshire. Although his father was against the idea at first, Franklin became a sailor on board a merchant ship when he was 12 years old. A year later, he joined the Royal Navy as a volunteer. After serving for only one year, he left in order to join the expedition of one of his uncles, Matthew Flinders, to the coast of Australia in 1802–1803. On his return, Franklin went into the Royal Navy once again and served in its ranks until the end of the Napoleonic Wars. He then expressed an interest in taking part in Arctic explorations.

Arctic explorer

In total, Franklin made four expeditions to the Arctic. During his second expedition (1819–22), he ran out of food and, to survive, the members were forced to eat the leather from their clothes and shoes. When Franklin returned to England, he became a national hero.

Franklin retired from Arctic exploration aged 39, having made maps of thousands of miles of coastline. However, 20 years later, the huge interest in finding a sea route to link the Atlantic and Pacific Oceans meant Franklin offered to lead another expedition.

Final expedition

Franklin took two well-equipped ships, the *Erebus* and the *Terror*. They set sail from Greenhithe in Kent on the 19th of May, 1845. On 26 July, the captain of a whaling ship saw them off the coast of Baffin Island. This is the last time the ships or the men were ever seen.

Thirty-nine separate expeditions set out to find Franklin and his crew, and slowly, evidence was found to explain the mystery of their disappearance. During the winter of 1846–47, the ships had become trapped in thick ice and even when summer came they were unable to escape.

In June 1847, Franklin died.

Questions

1 Why did Franklin leave the Royal Navy after one year's service? (*1 mark*)

2 Why did Franklin explore the Arctic before retiring at the age of 39? Tick your answer. (*1 mark*)

a to survey the Arctic and the Canadian coastline

b to learn about the Arctic peoples

c to find new species of fish and sea mammals

3 Why do you think Franklin became a national hero? (*3 marks*)

4 Why were other expeditions arranged to find Franklin and his ship? (*2 marks*)

5 Draw lines to join the dates to the correct events. (2 marks)

1786	Returned from second expedition to the Arctic
1798	Expedition to Australia
1802	Joined a merchant ship as a sailor
1822	Sir John Franklin died
1847	Sir John Franklin was born

6 Write a sentence to say why Sir John Franklin is remembered as a Great Explorer even though his last expedition ended tragically. (*3 marks*)

Where to next?

Since time began, humans have had a thirst for knowledge that lead to exploration. Many intrepid men and women have journeyed into the unknown and by doing so, increased our knowledge of the world.

In modern times, explorers have looked beyond our world and begun to explore space. This became known in the 1960s as the Space Race, as the USA and USSR competed to see who would be the first nation to land on the Moon.

Space Race

1957 Sputnik 1 was the first satellite to orbit the Earth. (USSR)

1959 Two monkeys, called Able and Baker, survived an orbit of the Earth. (USA)

1961 Yuri Gagarin was the first man to orbit the Earth. (USSR)

1963 Valentina Tereshkova became the first woman in space, orbiting the Earth 48 times and setting a new record. (USSR)

1968 The Apollo 8 spacecraft orbited the Moon ten times, manned by Frank Borman, James Lovell and William Anders. (USA)

1969 Neil Armstrong landed on the Moon in the lunar module 'Eagle' and became the first man to walk on its surface. He was followed by fellow astronaut Buzz Aldrin, while Michael Collins orbited the Moon in the mother ship 'Columbia'. (USA)

Since then, humans have built a permanent space station manned by astronauts from the USA, Russia (formerly USSR) and many other countries. They have also sent probes to Venus, Mars and Saturn and launched giant telescopes into space to explore even further than the earliest explorers would have dreamt of. Where do you think humans will go to next?

Questions

1 Which two countries competed in the Space Race? (*1 mark*)

2 Which country was the first to put a man into space? (*2 marks*)

3 Why do you think astronauts orbited the Earth before they orbited the Moon? (*3 marks*)

4 Write key words along the timeline to show the Space Race. (*2 marks*)

5 How does the author tell you that the USA and Russia are no longer competing in the Space Race? (*2 marks*)

6 Why do you think the author begins and ends the passage with a question? (*3 marks*)

Practice Writing Tests

Non-fiction

Long tasks

You have 45 minutes for your longer piece of writing, including up to 10 minutes of planning time. While planning, think about the PURPOSE and AUDIENCE. These are big clues to the type of text and features to use.

1. You think it might be fun to go exploring in an old disused quarry but your friend thinks it might be dangerous. Write the discussion you have about it with your friend.
2. You are on an adventure holiday with your school and have been potholing (exploring underground caves). Write a letter to your mother describing the day's events.
3. Your little sister wants to play one of your favourite computer games. Write an explanation that tells her what the purpose of the game is and how it works.

Short tasks

You have 20 minutes to plan, write and check your work.

1. A new space exploration programme is about to be announced, but there are not enough astronauts currently available. Write an advert to encourage more people to apply for a career as an astronaut.
2. While on an expedition you discover several new species of animal – the Bat-winged blue frog, the Giant flying stick insect, the Stub-toed pigeon owl, the Pygmy tiger. Write entries for an encyclopaedia about your discoveries.
3. You have donated a Pygmy tiger to a wildlife park. Write a set of instructions to tell them how to look after it.

Fiction

Long tasks

You have 45 minutes for your longer piece of writing, including up to 10 minutes of planning time.

1. Plan and write an adventure story with the title 'Lost in the Jungle'.
2. Plan and write a science-fiction story about a journey to a new planet.
3. Plan and write a fantasy story that features a hero, a dragon, a mysterious old man and a magic pool.

Short tasks

You have 20 minutes to plan, write and check your work.

1. You meet the famous explorer who will be leading the expedition to the North Pole. Write a description of your first impressions about him including character and appearance.
2. On your school adventure holiday, you are camping in a field. Write a description of it as you look out from your tent.
3. Write the opening paragraph for a short story about getting lost in a shopping centre.

Answers

Explore answers

Page 11
Connectives: after, first, then, and finally, soon, as, later, even

Page 15
Imperative verbs: put, build, fill, hang, add, remove, place, stir allow, pour, add

Page 19
Headings: answers will vary, e.g. introduction, place, home, food, appearance, song

Page 23
Connectives: time – today, so, first, because, now, which, cause

Page 27
Passive verb-phrases: are denied, has been found, will be improved, will be taken

Page 31
Connectives: although, until now, however, so, also, in conclusion

Page 38
Senses: sound, touch, sight

Page 39
Setting: morning or afternoon, birds crying, waves crashing, the railing

Page 40
Character: young, fit, spends time outdoors, bad-tempered, angry (confrontational, belligerent, unafraid)

Page 42
Themes: a) lost and found or good beats bad; b) good beats bad; c) wishing
Planning: Answers will vary.

Page 43
Planning: Answers will vary.

Sample writing task answers

Page 13

Question 1

Day 1

Arrived at last. What a long journey! Took ages to get here but what a blow. The camp had been wrecked in a storm. Though tired out, there was nothing for it but to set to and pitch the tents, etc. Late meal of tinned stew (ugh) and bed. Hope things are better tomorrow!

Question 2

Exclusive!

This newspaper is proud to be the first to bring you exclusive details about the journey to the jungle.

Edgar the Explorer (46) and six others in the group (John Smith, Pocahontas, Major Tom, Lord E. Lawdy, Daisy Chain and Matt Brown) set off on May 1st from Portsmouth on the first leg of their journey.

They embarked on *HMS Intrepid* for the long journey across the Atlantic Ocean. Despite being delayed by a hurricane in mid-ocean, the ship arrived only a day late on the South American continent.

The next stage of the journey was into the desert, where they travelled in a camel train for six days. Scorching sun by day and freezing nights did not dampen the spirits of the brave group.

Page 17

Question 1

How to make cheese on toast

Ingredients:
slice of white bread
grated cheese
brown sauce

Method:
1 Heat the grill.
2 Place the bread under the grill.
3 Grill until golden brown.
4 Remove from the grill.
5 Cover the ungrilled side with cheese and return to the grill.
6 Grill until the cheese bubbles and begins to brown slightly.
7 Remove from the grill and garnish with brown sauce.

Question 2

How to mend socks

You will need:
wool
darning needle
scissors

What you do:

First, cut a length of wool and thread the needle with it. Tie a small knot in one end of the wool. Now spread the hole in the sock over your fist. Thread the wool through one side of the hole and take it across to the other side. Next, thread the wool through the other side and return it to the first side. Continue until there is a criss-cross of wool over the hole. Now take the needle and thread it through the top of the hole. Take the wool down to the bottom edge by weaving in and out of the criss-cross of wool. Repeat the process until you have woven a patch across the hole. Finally make two or three small stitches to hold the wool in place and cut off the end.

Page 21

Question 1

The three-legged umbrella bird

This new species was discovered in the previously unexplored mountains of Peru by Edgar the Explorer in 2007. It is an exciting discovery as, instead of having wings, it 'flies' by catching the wind using its umbrella. It has three legs instead of the usual two, which help it to clamber up the trees to the top, where it finds the strongest winds.

The three-legged umbrella bird feeds on the nuts of the Mindle tree, a species of oak found only in Peru.

Question 2

Dearest Emily,

At last I have time to write and tell you all about the jungle here. It is a truly exciting place. The sights and sounds would amaze you.

The first thing that impressed me on arrival was the noise. It is never silent, especially at night. There are the calls of birds, the cries of monkeys and the rustle and creaking sounds of animals as they move around the undergrowth.

The plant life, too, is impressive. There are species of flower and tree that are completely new to me. I have found three new types of flower already!

There are several places to explore – the jungle floor, the tree canopy, and to one side, there are flat plains which look completely different to the jungle. We go there tomorrow.

I will write again when I have time and tell you all about it.

With all my love,

Edgar

Page 25

Question 1

Dear Mr Explorer,

The special containers I have sent to you will help you to bring home species without damage to them. They are made from clear plastic in a hexagonal shape, which means that you can pack them together in a box without wasting space. The plastic is lightweight, which also enables you to carry several boxes of containers at a time.

The lids are made from a new material which I invented. This is a fine membrane which allows air to circulate. This means that any live plants or animals will not suffocate and die on your return journey.

When you open the container's lid, taking care not to damage the membrane, and scoop a specimen inside, you will be able to watch it easily through the clear octagonal sides.

I hope your journey is a success and look forward to seeing what you bring home with you.

Yours sincerely,

Ian the Inventor

Question 2

How to row a boat

The person who rows a boat sits in the middle facing the back or stern. The oars are dipped into the water and the handles of the oars pulled towards the rower's chest. This makes the oar push through the water and results in the boat moving forwards. When the oar is lifted out, the boat will slow down again, so the action is repeated causing the boat to be propelled through the water.

Page 29

Question 1

Dear Sir Edgar,

I am writing to request that you include me in your expedition. Unfortunately, I cannot afford the fee, but I feel I would be a really useful member for many reasons.

I am very fit and healthy, so I would be able to help other children who are not as fit as I am. I am very cheerful too, so I could keep everyone's spirits up when times become difficult. I do not eat a lot, which means I would be a cheap member of the expedition. I also am very interested in discovering new things, and my enthusiasm would keep everyone keen. In short, I am fit, cheerful and very keen.

I urge you to consider my application and allow me to come with you. I am sure you won't regret it, and I will become the most valuable member of the team. I might even become a famous explorer like you!

Yours sincerely,

Hopeful Harry

Question 2

Come to the jungle!
Saturday 12th of May
St John's School is holding a jungle fair.
The children of St John's are raising money for an expedition to the jungle.
Come and experience:
Strange and exotic plants
Wonderful jungle scenes
Sounds and sights of the jungle
Only £2.00
2 p.m. to 6 p.m.

Page 33

Question 1

The problem we have is that we have lost the map.

Some of us think we should carry on. If we carry on, we might still find what we came for. We could make great discoveries and become heroes. But on the other hand, we might just go round in circles.

We could be lost, run out of food and die. Some of us think we should turn back. If we turn back we will have failed in our purpose. We will still have to find our way back without a map and could still get lost. However, we might be able to remember the way we came and save ourselves.

In summary, we need to decide which course is the best: to continue in the hope of success and possibly fail, or to turn back and possibly save our lives.

Question 2

The issue: should we try to find the Lost Tribes?

Points for	Points against
• We could learn how they have survived.	• We could take new germs and viruses to them.
• It will increase understanding about different types of people.	• We need to learn more about ourselves first.
• We might discover new resources.	• It would cost a great deal.

Reading comprehension

Page 51

The Wind Singer

1 domed huts
2 summer
3 silver ornaments
4 two of three – at the time, today, this was long before
5 They didn't answer questions.
6 to catch the wind

Page 53

Great Expectations

1 the churchyard
2 a forge
3 Joe Gargery
4 They were both bullied by Mrs Joe.
5 The stick was given a name.
6 He knows he will be beaten by the Tickler.

Page 55

Great Explorers

1 to join an expedition to Australia
2 answer A
3 Answers may vary, e.g. because he survived great hardship.
4 to find out what happened
5 1786 Franklin was born; 1798 joined merchant ship; 1802 expedition to Australia; 1822 returned from Arctic; 1847 Franklin died.
6 Answers will vary.

Page 57

Where to next?

1 USA and USSR
2 USSR
3 Answers will vary, e.g. sentences include the words less danger, easier, nearer.
4 Answers will vary.
5 The space station is manned by both countries.
6 Answers will vary, e.g. to make readers think.

Objectives

QCA writing assessment focus	Primary Framework for literacy strands and objectives	Title	Page no	Achieved (✓or ✗)
1 Write imaginative, interesting and thoughtful texts 2 Produce texts which are appropriate to task, reader and purpose	9 Creating and shaping texts • Write independently and creatively for purpose, pleasure and learning • Use and adapt a range of forms, suited to different purposes and readers • Make stylistic choices, including vocabulary, literacy features and viewpoint or voice • Use structural and presentational features for meaning and impact	Recount	10–13	
		Instructions	14–17	
		Non-chronological report	18–21	
		Explanation	22–25	
		Persuasion	26–29	
		Discussion	30–33	
		Setting	37–39	
		Characters and Themes	40–42	
		Practice Writing Tests	58–59	
3 Organise and present whole texts effectively, sequencing and structuring information, ideas and events 4 Construct paragraphs and use cohesion within and between paragraphs	10 Text structure and organisation • Organise ideas into a coherent structure, including layout, sections and paragraphs • Write cohesive paragraphs linking sentences within and between them	Recount	10–13	
		Instructions	14–17	
		Non-chronological reports	18–21	
		Explanation	22–25	
		Persuasion	26–29	
		Discussion	30–33	
		Setting description	37–39	
		Characters and Themes	40–42	
		Practice Writing Tests	58–59	
5 Vary sentences for clarity, purpose and effect 6 Write with technical accuracy of syntax and punctuation in phrases, clauses and sentences	11 Sentence structure and punctuation • Vary and adapt sentence structure for meaning and effect • Use a range of punctuation correctly to support meaning and emphasis • Convey meaning through grammatically accurate and correctly punctuated sentences	Recount	10–13	
		Instructions	14–17	
		Non-chronological report	18–21	
		Explanation	22–25	
		Persuasion	26–29	
		Discussion	30–33	
		Setting description	37–39	
		Characters and Themes	40–42	
		Practice Writing Tests	58–59	

<table>
<tr><th>QCA reading assessment focus</th><th>Primary Framework for literacy strands and objectives</th><th>Title</th><th>Page no</th><th>Achieved (✓or ✗)</th></tr>
<tr><td rowspan="4">2 Understand, describe, select or retrieve information, events or ideas from texts and use quotation and reference to text
3 Deduce, infer or interpret information, events or ideas from texts
4 Identify and comment on the structure and organisation of texts, including grammatical and presentational features at word and sentence level
5 Explain and comment on writers' uses of language</td><td rowspan="4">7 Understanding and interpreting texts
• Retrieve, select and describe information, events or ideas
• Deduce, infer and interpret information, events or ideas
• Use syntax, context, word structures and origins to develop their understanding of word meanings
• Identify and comment on the structure and organisation of texts
• Explain and comment on writers' use of language, including vocabulary, grammatical and literary features</td><td>The Wind Singer</td><td>50–51</td><td></td></tr>
<tr><td>Great Expectations</td><td>52–53</td><td></td></tr>
<tr><td>Great explorers</td><td>54–55</td><td></td></tr>
<tr><td>Where to next?</td><td>56–57</td><td></td></tr>
<tr><td rowspan="4">6 Identify and comment on writers' purposes and viewpoints and the overall effect on the reader</td><td rowspan="4">8 Engaging with and responding to texts
• Read independently for purpose, pleasure and learning
• Respond imaginatively, using different strategies to engage with texts
• Evaluate writers' purposes and viewpoints, and the overall effect of the text on the reader</td><td>The Wind Singer</td><td>50–51</td><td></td></tr>
<tr><td>Great Expectations</td><td>52–53</td><td></td></tr>
<tr><td>Great explorers</td><td>54–55</td><td></td></tr>
<tr><td>Where to next?</td><td>56–57</td><td></td></tr>
</table>